This library edition published in 2012 by Walter Foster Publishing, Inc.
Distributed by Black Rabbit Books.
P.O. Box 3263 Mankato, Minnesota 56002

Designed and published by Walter Foster Publishing, Inc.
© 2003 Disney Enterprises, Inc./ Pixar Animation Studios

Printed in Mankato, Minnesota, USA by CG Book Printers, a division of Corporate
Graphics.

First Library Edition

Library of Congress Cataloging-in-Publication Data

Parent, Nancy.
  Learn to draw Disney Pixar Finding Nemo : draw your favorite characters, step by
simple step / adapted by Nancy Parent ; illustrated by the Disney Storybook Artists.
-- 1st library ed.
      p. cm. -- (Learn to draw ; dc18l)
  ISBN 978-1-936309-34-4 (hardcover)
  1. Fishes in art--Juvenile literature. 2. Cartoon characters--Juvenile literature.
3. Drawing--Technique--Juvenile literature. 4. Finding Nemo (Motion picture)-
-Juvenile literature. 1. Pixar (Firm) II. Disney Storybook Artists. III. Title. IV. Title:
Disney Pixar Finding Nemo. V. Title: Draw your favorite characters, step by simple
step.
  NC1764.8.F57P373 2011
  741.5'1--dc22

                                                                   2011008876

042011
17320

9 8 7 6 5 4 3 2 1

Learn to Draw

DISNEY · PIXAR

FINDING NEMO

Draw your favorite characters, step by simple step

Adapted by
Nancy Parent

Illustrated
by the Disney
Storybook
Artists

Walter Foster

Walter Foster Publishing, Inc.
3 Wrigley, Suite A
Irvine, CA 92618
www.walterfoster.com

The Story of

Hi! My name is Marlin—you know, Nemo's father. I'm here to tell you a story. It's all about finding my son . . . finding Nemo. Years ago, Coral, my dear wife, and I were watching over our hundreds of eggs in our new home at the Drop-off. Suddenly a barracuda attacked, and Coral and all the eggs were taken from me. I was devastated. Then I saw one tiny damaged egg left. I named the newborn Nemo and promised I would never let anything happen to him.

Nemo is a great little guy, despite the fact that when he was younger he was much too curious and adventurous for an overprotective father like me. He was born with one damaged fin, which I called his "lucky" fin. Unfortunately this lucky fin kept him from being a great swimmer. And that made me worry even more.

I kept Nemo out of school for as long as I could, but I finally had to give in. After all, I couldn't send a teenager off to first grade! On the first day of school, I thought I would be okay until I learned that their first field trip was going to the dangerous Drop-off! I raced after the class and found Nemo at the edge of the deep water!

I admit I panicked. I embarrassed poor Nemo so much that he felt he had to prove he was brave and strong. Before I knew it, he was swimming out to the deep water. He tagged a boat, impressing his new school friends. But then something terrible happened: A scuba diver swam up behind my son and netted him!

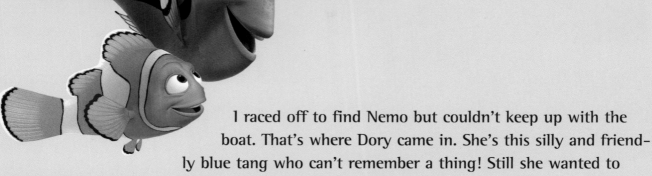

I raced off to find Nemo but couldn't keep up with the boat. That's where Dory came in. She's this silly and friendly blue tang who can't remember a thing! Still she wanted to help, and I was grateful. She even came up with our first clue. You see, Dory read the address on the diver's mask that ended up on the ocean floor. It said: P. Sherman, 42 Wallaby Way, Sydney.

Meanwhile Nemo was stuck in a fish tank in P. Sherman's dental office in Sydney. Nemo made friends with a group of goofy fish, and when they learned that the dentist was going to give Nemo to his niece Darla, they quickly set up a plan to save him. You see, Darla was bad news for fish. She liked to shake them to death!

The tank's leader, Gill, thought up a plan for the tank fish to escape to the ocean. They were going to make the tank as dirty as possible so the dentist would have to clean it. That meant taking the fish out of the tank and putting them in plastic bags on the counter. From there, they would hop in their bags over to the window and jump into the harbor. (Why didn't they just serve themselves up on skewers and leap onto the barbecue? And they call *me* a "clownfish!")

Anyway Gill took Nemo under his fin to help him become a stronger swimmer. But their plan was foiled when the dentist installed a brand-new filter that was guaranteed to keep the tank clean . . . no matter how hard the fish tried to make it dirty.

Back in the ocean, Dory and I had finally reached Sydney Harbor after some pretty harrowing adventures of our own—including run-ins with a hungry shark, a vicious anglerfish, and an almost-deadly forest of stinging jellyfish. The best part was meeting this cool turtle named "Crush" who rescued us after we escaped the jellyfish. He had the cutest little son named "Squirt" who reminded me of Nemo.

Then, when we got to the harbor, a pelican tried to eat us for breakfast! But I figured I had traveled so far to find Nemo that I wasn't about to give up. I fought like crazy. We were coughed up and picked up off the dock by another pelican named Nigel. Somehow he knew my story and took us right to the dentist's office. I was going to find my son!

Little did we know that Darla had arrived, ready for her present. The dentist scooped Nemo into a little plastic bag. But Nemo tricked the guy by playing dead. The tank fish realized Nemo was trying the "toilet escape"—he would get flushed down the toilet and make his way to the ocean. The fish were ecstatic . . . until the dentist headed for the trash can!

When Dory, Nigel, and I got there, I saw Nemo, looking dead as could be, floating in that little plastic bag. I was overcome with grief. I had no idea the little guy was actually still alive! The dentist pushed Nigel out the window, and the friendly pelican took Dory and me back to the harbor.

Meanwhile the tank fish launched Gill out of the tank to save Nemo. He hit a dental mirror that Nemo was resting on and sent Nemo flying into the spit sink and down the drain into the harbor!

Minutes later Dory ran into Nemo in the harbor. I had already left Dory because I was so sad that I wanted to be alone. It took her a little while to recognize Nemo, but when she did, they raced off together until they found me! But then a huge fishing net came down and trapped a bunch of fish, including Dory! Nemo got an idea. If the fish "swam down," they could pull on the net and break free. Nemo wanted to get into the net with the doomed fish to help them! I was beside myself—I had finally found my son, and now he wanted to risk his life! Well I finally let him go, and it worked! The fish were freed, and Nemo and I shared a really happy reunion. Dory joined right in.

When Dory, Nemo, and I made our way home to the reef, Nemo was excited about going back to school. And this time, I was ready to let him go.

Oh, and by the way, last I heard, Nemo's tank friends were floating in little plastic bags in the harbor. Seems Gill's escape plan finally worked. . . .

Tools and Materials

In the following section, you're going to meet a group of fishy characters that will be a lot of fun to draw! Let me tell you, it should be a lot easier for you to draw them than for me to cross the treacherous ocean! There's nothing like a good graphite pencil, some colored markers, and watercolor or acrylic paints when it comes to drawing and coloring us fish. We're a pretty colorful bunch, so go a little crazy—the brighter the better, as far as I'm concerned!

graphite pencil and paper

sharpener

eraser

felt-tip markers

paintbrush and paints

colored pencils

Ready?

Let's start with the basics. Just follow these simple steps, and you'll be amazed at how fun and easy drawing can be.

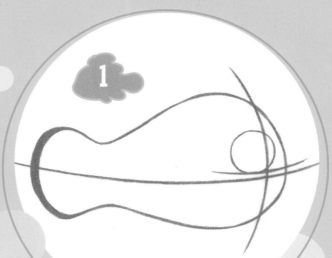

Step 1
Draw the basic shape of the character. Then add some simple guidelines to help you place the features.

Step 2
Each new step appears in blue.

Step 3
Simply follow the blue lines to add the details.

Step 4
Now darken the lines you want to keep and erase the rest.

Step 5
Use crayons, colored pencils, paints, or markers to add vivid colors.

 N e m o

Clownfish

You remember Nemo. He's my son—the adventurous little fish with the "lucky" fin who longs for excitement and friends to play with. But instead, he's saddled with me, an overprotective single dad who never lets the poor little guy out of sight.

Well, one day, Nemo dares to show his friends he's not scared of the ocean (the way his dad is), and he swims off alone. He ends up getting a lot more excitement than he bargained for! But he also discovers just how brave and resourceful he can be. That's my boy!

from side, Nemo is shaped like Goldfish® cracker

from front, body looks like gumdrop

"lucky" fin is wedge-shaped with notch cut out

YES! rays follow curve of fin

NO! too straight and even

YES! varied stripe shapes

NO! too similar and too straight

YES! top (dorsal) fin is 2 different shapes pointing at different angles

NO! too even; too upright

Nemo is about 4 "eyes tall" including top fin

top fin is same height as 1 eye

YES! bottom fins are set apart from each other

NO! fins look like bow tie

3

4

5

Marlin

Clownfish

I'm that not-so-funny clownfish, Marlin (Nemo's dad). After losing almost all my family, I sort of become crazy about doing everything possible to keep my only son safe from the dangerous ocean. Unfortunately I go a little overboard and don't allow Nemo to do anything—I don't even let him go to school!

I fuss and fret a lot, but I really do mean well. It takes a little journey across the ocean, and meeting up with Dory, to teach me the meaning of trust and letting go. When it comes down to it, I'm just a regular dad who will do anything for his son.

Marlin is about 2 times the size of Nemo

rays on Marlin's fins
and tail radiate out
from "meaty" parts
of body like this . . .

"meaty" parts

. . . not like this

face is kind
of flat

5 rays on side
(pectoral) fins
and tail

from side, shaped
like turkey
drumstick

bags under
eyes make
him look tired

YES!
eyes close
together

NO! eyes
too far apart

3

4

5

Dory

Regal Blue Tang

Dory is one chatty, friendly, funny fish! She never gives up hope—when things get tough, she just keeps on swimming. Always willing and helpful, Dory has everything going for her except for one small thing—her memory. She can't remember anything! But she risks her own life to help me find Nemo (despite the fact that she can't remember the little guy's name!).

from front, Dory's stripe defines where "eyebrows" end

freckles follow curved bridge of "nose"

YES! curved freckle pattern

NO! too straight

Dory is just over 4 times the size of Nemo

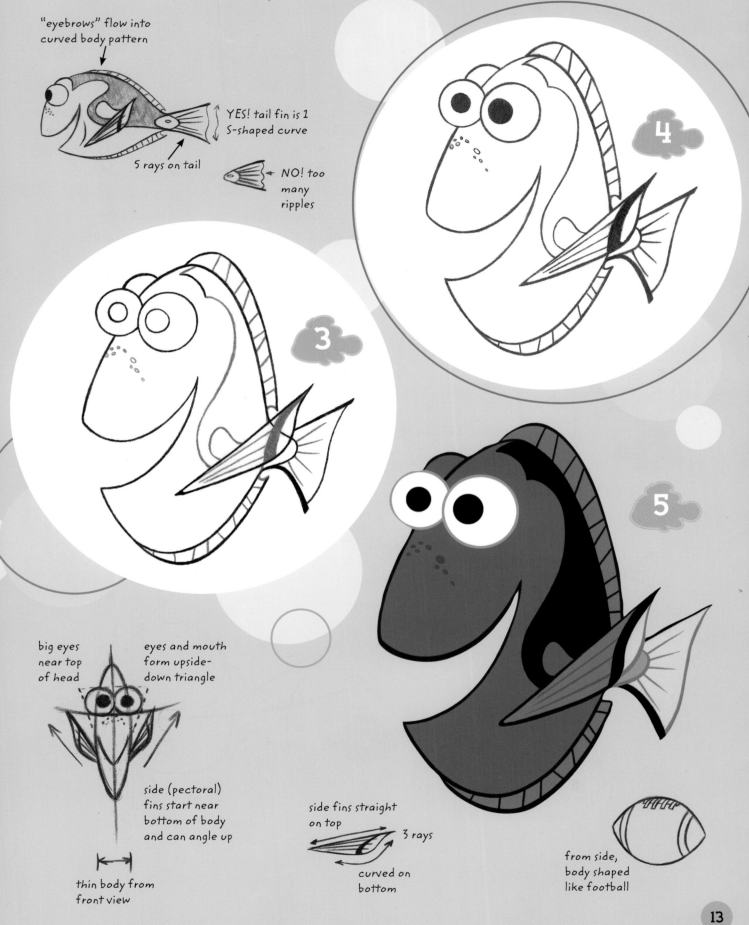

"eyebrows" flow into
curved body pattern

YES! tail fin is 1
S-shaped curve

5 rays on tail

NO! too
many
ripples

3

4

5

big eyes
near top
of head

eyes and mouth
form upside-
down triangle

side (pectoral)
fins start near
bottom of body
and can angle up

thin body from
front view

side fins straight
on top

3 rays

curved on
bottom

from side,
body shaped
like football

13

Gill

Moorish Idol

Gill is the leader of the tank fish—a group of fish trapped in a tank in a dentist's office. According to Nemo, Gill is charming, likable, tough, and determined to break his friends out of the tank. He takes Nemo under his "scarred" fin to teach him the ropes and gives Nemo a part to play in the great escape he's been planning for years. Gill is a dreamer, a believer, and a doer, and I'll always be grateful to him.

Gill is about 14 times the size of Nemo

YES! big, blocky eyebrows

eyes usually half closed

one line under each eye

NO! brows are too thin

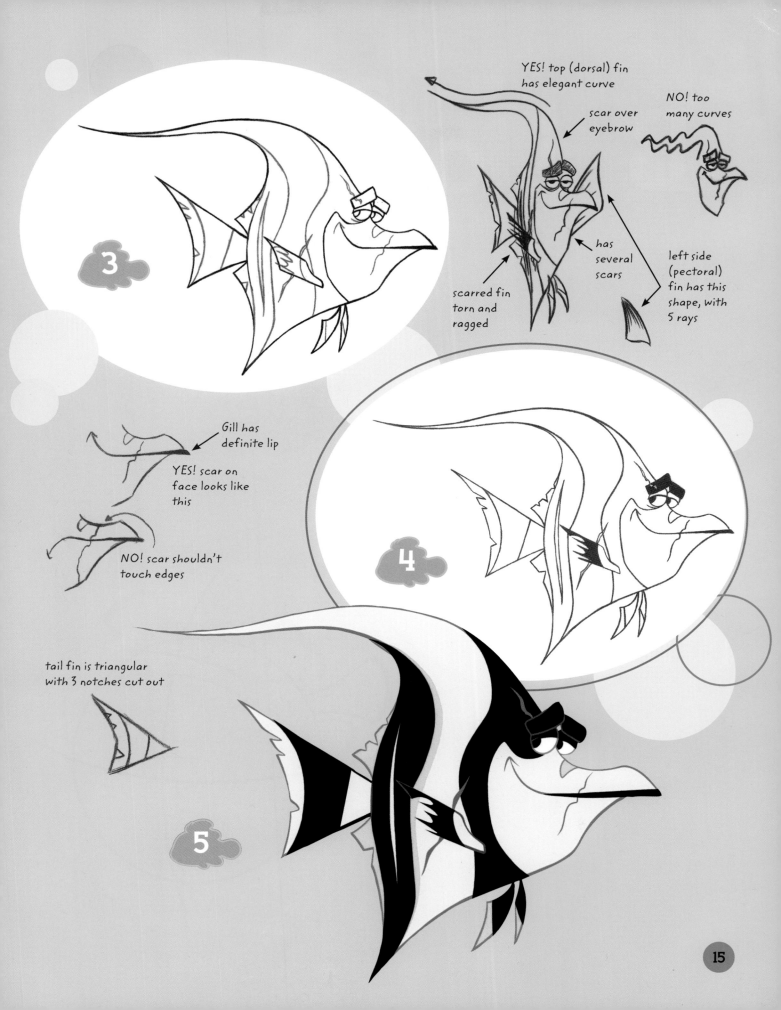

YES! top (dorsal) fin has elegant curve

NO! too many curves

scar over eyebrow

has several scars

scarred fin torn and ragged

left side (pectoral) fin has this shape, with 5 rays

Gill has definite lip

YES! scar on face looks like this

NO! scar shouldn't touch edges

tail fin is triangular with 3 notches cut out

3

4

5

Bloat

Blowfish

Bloat is a blowfish who holds it together until he can't take it anymore. Then he literally blows up like a balloon. He is Gill's trusted lieutenant in running the tank business. However the stress of living in the tank often gets to him. Poor guy!

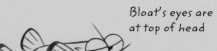

Bloat's eyes are at top of head

big underbite

YES! when Bloat isn't puffed out, "spikes" follow action of body and point toward tail

NO! spikes too upright

1

2

Bloat is about 4 times the size of Nemo (when he's not puffed out or "bloated")

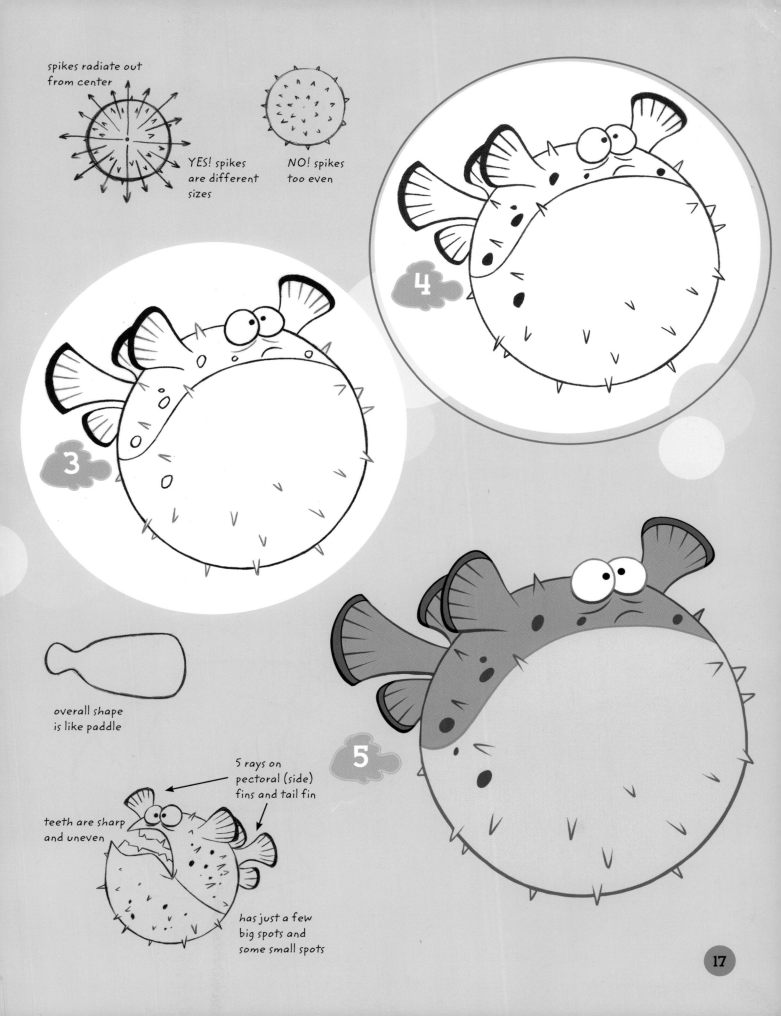

spikes radiate out from center

YES! spikes are different sizes

NO! spikes too even

3

4

overall shape is like paddle

5

5 rays on pectoral (side) fins and tail fin

teeth are sharp and uneven

has just a few big spots and some small spots

Bubbles

Yellow Tang

Did you ever hear the saying, "life is just a bowl of bubbles?" Well for Bubbles, it is. This crazy fish is in love with bubbles. He faithfully waits for bubbles to burst from the tank's plastic treasure chest and then joyously scrambles to put them back in. He never tires of this game, and he keeps the other fish amused. For Bubbles, it's all about the bubbles.

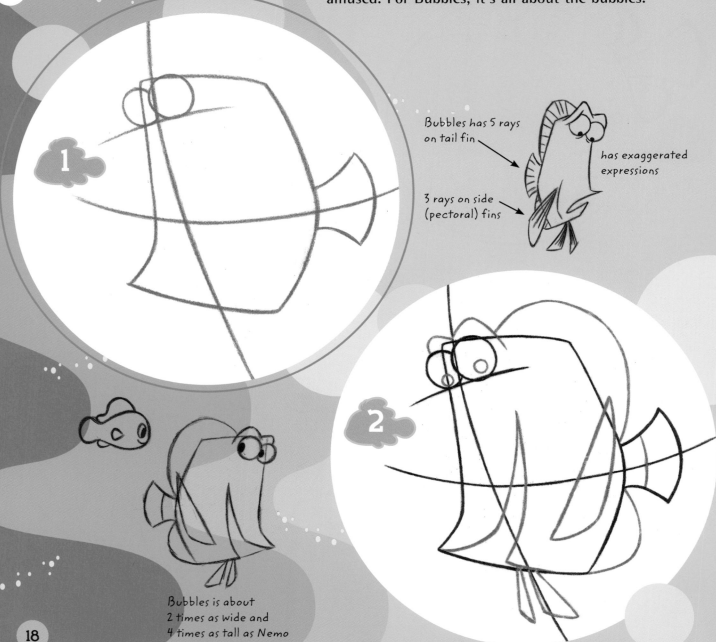

Bubbles has 5 rays on tail fin

has exaggerated expressions

3 rays on side (pectoral) fins

Bubbles is about 2 times as wide and 4 times as tall as Nemo

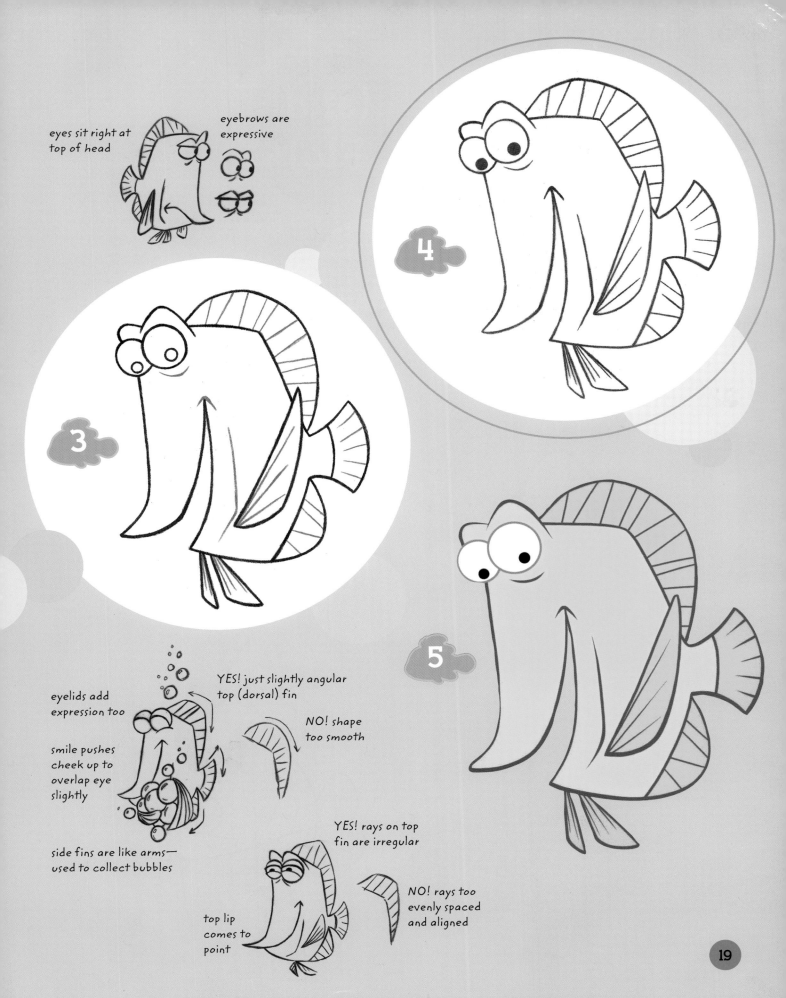

eyes sit right at top of head

eyebrows are expressive

4

3

5

eyelids add expression too

YES! just slightly angular top (dorsal) fin

NO! shape too smooth

smile pushes cheek up to overlap eye slightly

side fins are like arms— used to collect bubbles

top lip comes to point

YES! rays on top fin are irregular

NO! rays too evenly spaced and aligned

19

Deb (and Flo)

Black-and-White Humbug

Next we have Deb and her twin sister, Flo. The two of them are inseparable. They go everywhere and do everything together. They joke, swim, and tell secrets—but only to each other. They look and act exactly alike. In fact, they are so much alike that one would think they were one and the same fish—which they are. Are you following this? You see, the tank fish don't have the heart to tell Deb that Flo is her reflection in the tank glass.

Deb talks to her own reflection

Deb is about 2 times the size of Nemo

body is triangle-shaped

shape and stripes look like volcano

YES! top (dorsal) fin has tousled-hair look

NO! too sharp and rigid

keep lips somewhat thin

heart-shaped tail fin

Gurgle

Royal Gramma

Here's a guy after my own heart. His name is Gurgle. Gurgle is a fussy little fish who refuses to touch anything around him. He's so afraid of germs that he is completely obsessed with them. He believes that if he steers clear of everything and everyone in the tank, his odds are better for a longer, happier life. How smart is that! Everybody knows that tank fish don't live forever, and Gurgle isn't taking any chances!

Gurgle's body curves like an oblong water balloon

Gurgle is about 2 times the size of Nemo

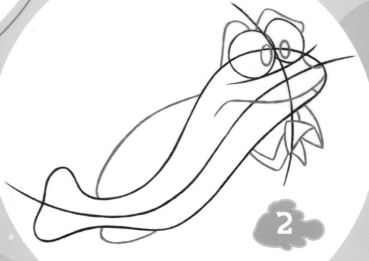

eyes sit on top of head

YES! lips
are angular

NO! lips
too rounded

YES! rounded
tail fin

NO! tail fin
too pointed

if flat, pattern would
look like this . . .

. . . but on body,
pattern curves
as if wrapped
around tube

YES! pupils are oval

NO! pupils too round

pupils get smaller
when he's scared

Peach

Starfish

Meet Peach—the tank's star reporter. She spends day after day stuck up high on the glass wall of that tank. And what else is there to do but report back on everything she sees? Unfortunately life can be pretty boring in a dentist's office, except when the dentist is working on a patient. Peach has watched countless hours of dental procedures, so she is the tank's dental expert. She spends the rest of her days counting floor tiles and watching the plants die.

1

Peach's reflection shows on glass as she pulls away

2

Peach is about 3 times the size of Nemo

YES! angles and
points are rounded

NO! too sharp

3

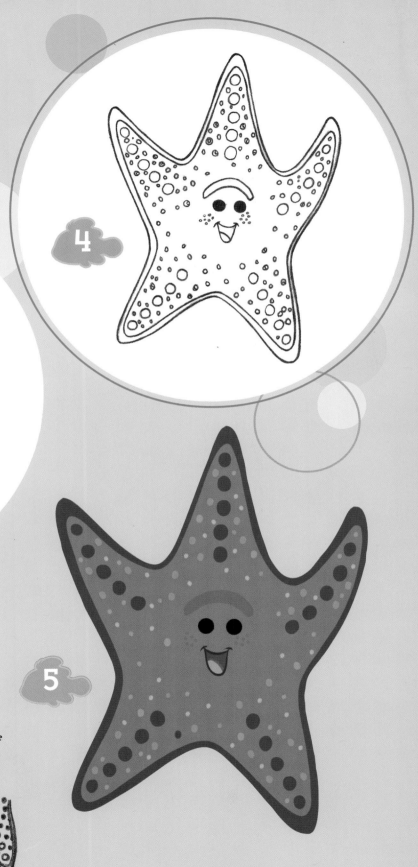

4

star points
work like
arms and legs

eyes are solid
black circles

YES! small spots are
various sizes and in
uneven pattern

5 main circles for
suctions on each
arm (inside)

NO! spots
too even

eyebrows and
shape of eyes show
her expression

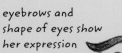

5

Jacques

Cleaner Shrimp

Jacques is a true original. He is one shrimp who loves to clean. He would clean the tank from morning until night if he could. I can see where cleaning could help a fish relax a little. After all, I like a nice clean reef myself! Jacques is like a good soldier: he's a born fighter, always doing battle with his greatest enemy—tank scum.

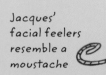

Jacques' facial feelers resemble a moustache

1

Jacques is just half the size of Nemo

2

YES! eyes overlap

 NO! too far apart

legs spiky and notched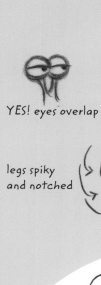

"hands" are like mitts

4

3

tail fin has 1 large spot and 2 small ones

 YES! thin dark stripes

 NO! dark stripes too thick

body always curves

5

Sharks

Chum – Mako
Anchor – Hammerhead
Bruce – Great White

Now even I have a hard time with these fellows. Meet Bruce, Anchor, and Chum—three good friends who are inseparable. Anchor is the moody one who hates dolphins. Chum is always on the go; he just can't keep still. And Bruce is the happy-go-lucky leader of the pack. These sharks want to be friends with everyone under the sea. The only problem is, when we other fish see them coming, we all go swimming! Who knew they'd given up eating us? They've even formed a support group, and they have meetings to help promote their vegetarian lifestyle. Good luck, fellas!

1

2

Chum

3

Chum's overall shape is like long, sharp knife

YES! angled eye shape

NO! eye too straight and square

28

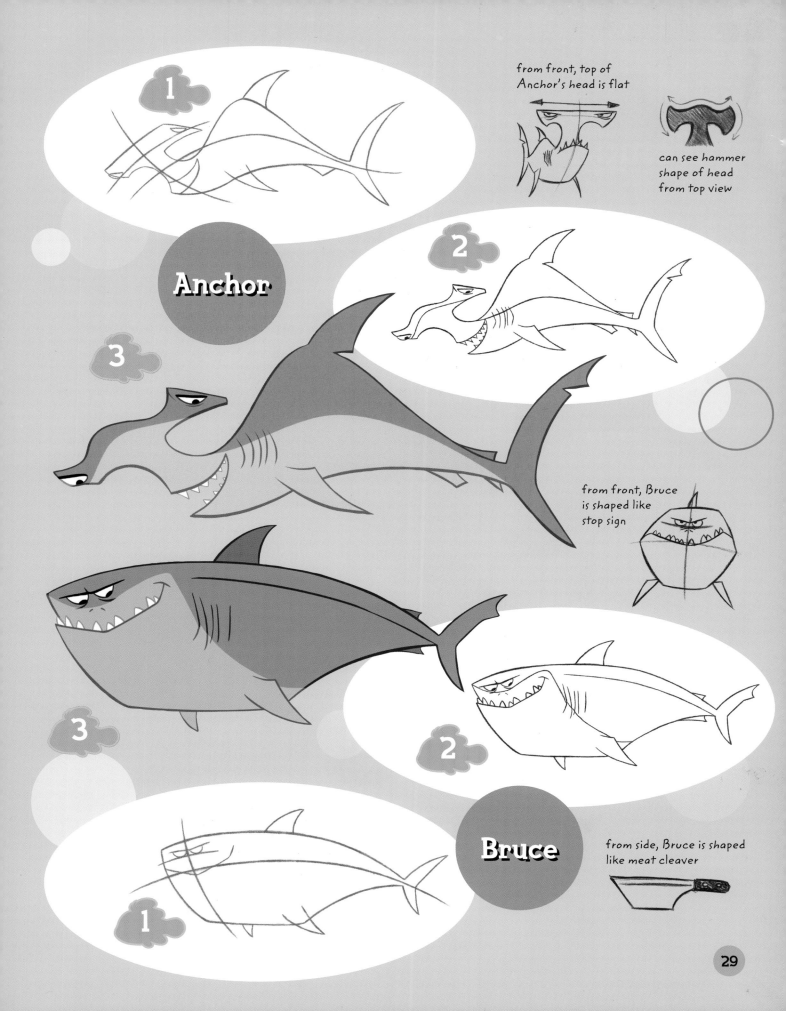

1

from front, top of Anchor's head is flat

can see hammer shape of head from top view

Anchor

2

3

from front, Bruce is shaped like stop sign

3

2

Bruce

from side, Bruce is shaped like meat cleaver

Nemo's School Friends

Here are three of Nemo's school friends he'd like you to meet: First there's Tad, the leader of this trio. He describes himself as "obnoxious" because he likes to have fun *and* cause trouble. Then there's Pearl, who always says exactly what's on her mind. She loves twirling those eight long tentacles of hers and doing fancy tricks. Finally there's Sheldon. He likes to gallop around the reef with his pals, but he has a hard time playing tag. You see, Sheldon is H_2O-intolerant, so he's constantly sneezing, and the force sends him flying off backward! That's why he's always the last one to "touch base."

Tad – Long-Nosed Butterfly Fish
Pearl – Flapjack Octopus
Sheldon – Sea Horse

1

Tad

2

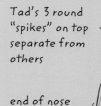

3

Tad and Pearl are about 1-1/2 times Nemo's size

Sheldon is about the same size as Nemo

Tad's 3 round "spikes" on top separate from others

end of nose turns up

pointed tail

Pearl

1

2

3

Pearl's "topknot" looks like a hair ribbon

"legs" curve with movement

Sheldon

1

2

3

Sheldon's tail has soft curve on inside and hard edge on outside

YES! sharp outside angle

NO! too round

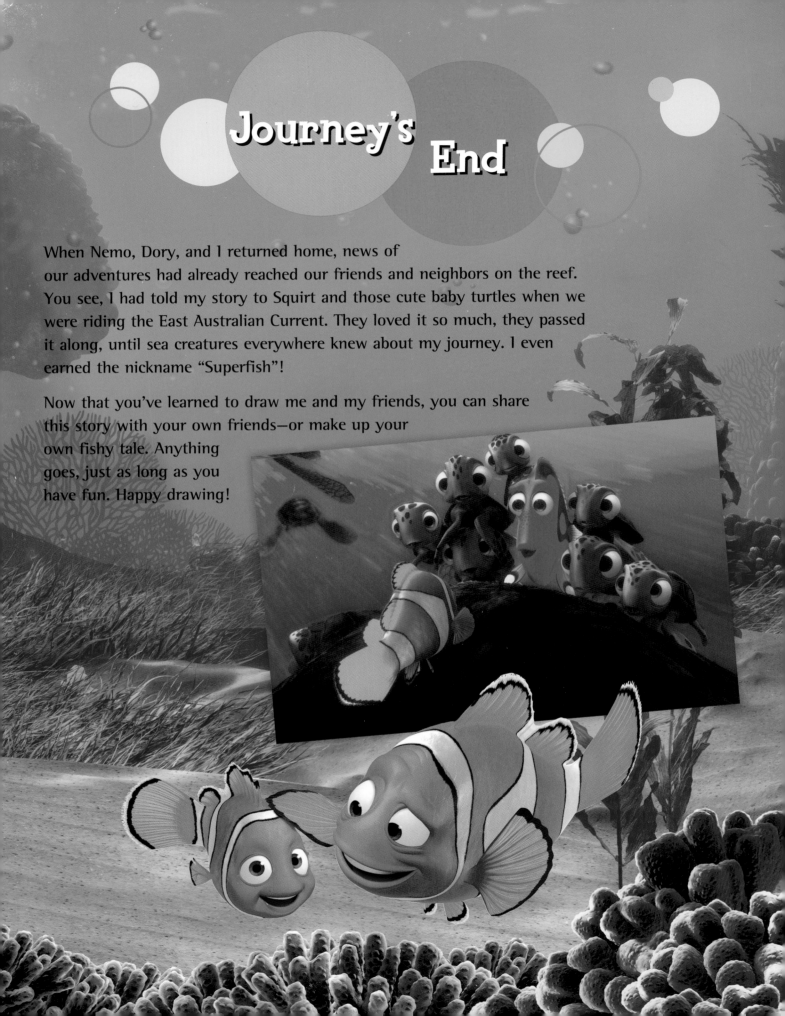

Journey's End

When Nemo, Dory, and I returned home, news of
our adventures had already reached our friends and neighbors on the reef.
You see, I had told my story to Squirt and those cute baby turtles when we
were riding the East Australian Current. They loved it so much, they passed
it along, until sea creatures everywhere knew about my journey. I even
earned the nickname "Superfish"!

Now that you've learned to draw me and my friends, you can share
this story with your own friends—or make up your
own fishy tale. Anything
goes, just as long as you
have fun. Happy drawing!